BEFORE I MADE HISTORY™

Let's Fly, Wilbur and Orville!

by Peter and Connie Roop

SCHOLASTIC INC.

New York   Toronto   London   Auckland   Sydney
Mexico City   New Delhi   Hong Kong   Buenos Aires

D0019012

For Mother, whose heart soars with love

ISBN 0-439-55441-1

Text copyright © 2003 by Peter and Connie Roop.
Illustrations copyright © 2003 by Scholastic Inc.
All rights reserved. Published by Scholastic Inc.
SCHOLASTIC and associated logos are trademarks and/or registered trademarks of Scholastic Inc.

12 11 10   6 7 8/0

Printed in the U.S.A.   40
First printing, September 2003

Table of Contents

Introduction   1

1. Wilbur Wright   3

2. Orville Wright   8

3. Wilbur and Orville Learn
   and Earn   13

4. Orville's Ideas   19

5. The Wright Brothers'
   Printing Business   24

6. The Wright Brothers'
   Bicycle Business   31

7. Why Not Fly?   37

8. Kitty Hawk   42

9. First Flight   48

10. Wilbur and Orville Fly
    Into History   54

Introduction

Wilbur and Orville Wright are famous. They invented the first airplane. Do you know something you use that they invented before the airplane?

Wilbur and Orville's mother liked to build things, too. Do you know what toy she made for her children?

The Wright brothers built airplanes as adults. Do you know what flying toys they built when they were young?

Wilbur and Orville were excellent athletes. Do you know what sports they played?

The Wright brothers never graduated from high school. But did you know that they both received college degrees?

The Wright brothers built many toys as

adults. Do you know what toy taught them the most about flying?

Wilbur and Orville chose to fly their first airplane in Kitty Hawk, North Carolina. Do you know why they picked Kitty Hawk?

Wilbur and Orville had to decide who would be the first to fly in their airplane. Do you know how they decided?

Wilbur and Orville Wright received medals for their airplane work. Do you know that another Wright child also received a special medal for helping them?

The answers to these questions lie in who Wilbur and Orville Wright were as boys and as young men. This book is about Wilbur and Orville Wright before they made history.

1
Wilbur Wright

On April 16, 1867, a spring breeze blew across the Wright farm in Millville, Indiana. Inside the farmhouse, a baby cried. Milton and Susan Wright smiled. Their third son, Wilbur, had been born.

The Wrights gave their children unusual first names. Reuchlin Wright was born in 1861. His nickname was Roosh. Lorin Wright was born in 1862. To honor Wilbur Fiske, a friend, the Wrights named their third son Wilbur. Wilbur Wright was a name that would one day soar into history.

When he was ten months old, Wilbur walked. He tottered into a room and zoomed toward anything that made him curious. His father said that Wilbur was the first to find the greatest mischief!

Reverend Wright was a minister in the United Brethren Church. In 1868, when Wilbur was one year old, his father became a professor of church history. The Wrights moved to Hartsville, Indiana. This was the first of many moves for Wilbur. His father's duties required him to move often.

Reverend Wright enjoyed reading, writing, and learning. He told stories, gave talks, and wrote articles. He kept a daily journal, a habit he passed on to his children.

Reverend Wright had many strong beliefs. He was pleased slavery had ended. He believed in tight-knit families. He wanted equal rights for women. He believed girls and boys should have equal opportunities for an education. Reverend Wright passed these beliefs on to his children.

Mrs. Wright was a quiet, loving mother. She worked hard at home, cooking, cleaning, and caring for her children. Mrs. Wright was extremely shy and focused her energy on her family. Mrs. Wright loved to do things with her hands. She sewed her own clothes. She made toys for her boys. One winter, Mrs. Wright even built a sled for her sons! Mrs. Wright learned her handy skills from her father, John Koerner, who made carriages.

The Wright children went to their mother when something broke because she could fix anything. Reverend Wright hardly knew which end of a hammer to hold!

The Wrights encouraged their children to be creative, to marvel at the world and understand it. When the Wright boys took something apart to see how it worked, their parents didn't mind. They showed the children respect and great patience.

Both parents wanted their children to learn. Mrs. Wright had gone to college. This was unusual for a woman in the 1800s. She did very well, especially in math. Her children inherited her math skills.

When Wilbur was two years old, the family moved to Dayton, Ohio. On March 7, 1870, when he was almost three years old,

Wilbur was excited. His mother had twins named Otis and Ida! Sadly, both babies died. The Wrights remembered their twins, especially on their birthday.

In April 1871, when Wilbur was four years old, the Wrights bought a white house at 7 Hawthorn Street in Dayton. Here, Wilbur spent many happy years of his life.

The two-story house on Hawthorn Street was brand-new. There was also a barn, a shed, and an outhouse. A pump provided the Wrights with clean, cool water. In those days, many people got sick from drinking polluted water. All his life, Wilbur was careful about the water he drank.

There were four bedrooms in the new Wright home. In the parents' front bedroom, on August 19, 1871, Orville Wright was born. Wilbur was four years old when Orville was born. One day these brilliant brothers would change the world.

2
Orville Wright

Orville Wright was named after the Unitarian minister Orville Dewey. Reverend and Mrs. Wright respected Reverend Dewey very much.

Orville took his first steps when he was one year old. He was curious about his home and eagerly explored it. When Orville saw something that interested him, he went straight to it, just like Wilbur had done.

Orville enjoyed watching his big brothers play and do things. Roosh and Lorin, the oldest children, played and studied together. Wilbur wanted to be with his older brothers. Sometimes Wilbur played tag with the big boys, but only if he was "it."

One day when Wilbur was five years old,

Roosh and Lorin wanted to go swimming. They didn't want Wilbur tagging along. Wilbur shouted, "I'll squall!" After this, when his big brothers wouldn't let Wilbur do something, Wilbur yelled, "I'll squall!" Wilbur usually got his way.

Orville had a big surprise on his third birthday, August 19, 1874. His sister, Katharine, was born! Katharine was named after her grandmother, Catherine Koerner. The Wrights changed the spelling so that Katharine's name would be as special as her brothers'. Katharine and Orville enjoyed sharing the same birthday.

The Wrights were like two families. Roosh and Lorin did things together. Sometimes they let Wilbur join them. Orville and Katharine played together. Orville pulled Katharine in his wagon. He invited her to play neighborhood games.

Wilbur enjoyed telling stories to Orville and Katharine. Wilbur's funny stories always ended with "and then the boiler burst!"

Wilbur teased Orville and Katharine just

as Roosh and Lorin had teased him. If Orville said a word wrong, Wilbur teased him until Orville got so mad he would throw a rock at Wilbur. Wilbur made Katharine cry by pointing at her and making an angry face.

Wilbur, Orville, and Katharine loved one another. They had their own special nicknames. Wilbur was Ullum, Orville was Bubo, and Katharine was Swes.

Wilbur and Orville became close friends. Wilbur wrote, "From the time we were little children, my brother Orville and myself lived together, played together, worked together, and, in fact, thought together." They even owned their toys together! Later, the Wright brothers would share their business, their money, and their dream of flying.

Orville went to kindergarten when he was five years old. He quickly learned the way to school. He could walk to school by himself, but he had to be home for lunch.

Orville did not like kindergarten. After a few days, he pretended to go to school. But instead, Orville went to the home of his best friend, Ed Sines. All morning, Orville and Ed played. Orville knew how to tell time, so he hurried home just before lunch.

After a month, Mrs. Wright went to school to see how Orville was doing. "I hope the child is behaving himself," Mrs. Wright said to the teacher. Mrs. Wright knew Orville's energy could get him into trouble.

The teacher said, "Why, you know, since the first few days, I haven't seen him."

Mrs. Wright decided to teach Orville at home. She and Mr. Wright wanted their children to be well educated.

In 1877, when he was six years old, Orville got into big trouble. Orville and Ed Sines built a fire by a fence. Katharine watched them. Suddenly, the fire grew bigger, and the boys couldn't stop it. Katharine ran to get Mrs. Wright, who put out the fire. The Wrights did not spank their children very often, but Orville surely must have been punished.

3
Wilbur and Orville
Learn and Earn

The Wrights were not poor, but they had little money to spare for extra things. If Wilbur and Orville wanted something, they had to earn the money.

Wilbur usually saved his money. Orville usually spent his money. Orville often borrowed money from Wilbur, who made sure his little brother paid him back.

The boys had regular chores to do, like shoveling coal, chopping wood, and keeping the wood box filled. Mrs. Wright paid them a penny to dry dishes. Orville was creative in how he earned extra money. Once he collected old animal bones and sold them to a fertilizer factory. This was hard work. Orville made only three pennies a load!

Reverend Wright believed toys would spark his children's imagination. When Orville turned five, he was given an unusual present called a gyroscope. This toy spun like a top, but it could balance on a knife-edge. Orville spun and spun his new toy, trying to figure out how it worked. Wilbur was also interested in the gyroscope.

In 1877, Reverend Wright was elected bishop of their church. Unfortunately, being bishop meant he had to visit many churches. Some years he traveled eight thousand miles!

In June 1878, the Wrights rented out their Hawthorn Street home and moved to Adams Street in Cedar Rapids, Iowa. Wilbur was eleven years old, and Orville was six.

Wilbur and Orville liked Cedar Rapids. The town was small, and they soon made new friends. Orville quickly became a neighborhood leader. He was the general of an army of his friends. When Orville told his mother about their adventures, he got so excited he almost fell out of his chair!

Wilbur did not get so excited about things. He was more serious. He took his time when making decisions.

All their lives, Wilbur studied before acting, while Orville's energy and ideas kept them involved in unusual projects.

When Wilbur was eleven years old and Orville was seven, they enrolled in Jefferson Elementary School. Mrs. Wright hoped that Orville would behave himself in school now that he was older.

Later that fall, Bishop Wright came home with a special present. It was an unusual toy made of paper and bamboo, with four propellers and a rubber band.

Bishop Wright wound up the rubber band and let the toy go. Instead of falling to the floor, the toy zoomed to the ceiling. Wilbur and Orville had never seen a flying machine!

They played and played with the toy. They took it apart to see how it worked. They built copies of the toy using bamboo,

paper, cork, and rubber bands. Orville wrote, "We built a number of copies of this toy which flew successfully." In second grade, Orville got in trouble for making a copy of the toy in school!

The Wright brothers decided to build a bigger, better toy. They experimented with longer propellers. But no matter how hard they tried, their heavy toy wouldn't fly. The Wright brothers had a lot to learn about flying machines.

Wilbur worked hard in school and got good grades. He sometimes daydreamed but rarely got in trouble. Wilbur liked geography, history, and math.

In second grade, Orville won a prize for his excellent handwriting. He liked to read so much that he set out to prove he should be using the third-grade reading book. To go to the third-grade book, Orville had to read a difficult part of the second-grade book.

Orville worked hard to get every word right. When the time came for him to read,

Orville sped through the book. Even though he was holding it upside down, he passed!

Orville told his parents that he was a third-grade reader. Bishop Wright said, "Well, that's a strange thing. Just this morning I bought the third reader you asked for." Orville had been confident of his success!

When Bishop Wright traveled, he wrote long letters home. He expected letters back. In 1880, when Orville was nine years old, he wrote on a postcard to his father, "My teacher said I was a good boy today." This was wonderful news, because Orville was often in trouble at school.

He also wrote about an experiment he tried at home. "The other day I took a can and filled it with water. Then I put it on the stove. I waited a little while and the water came squirting out of the top about a foot." Mrs. Wright was very patient with her youngest son.

4
Orville's Ideas

By 1881, Wilbur was fourteen years old, and Orville was ten. Bishop Wright had grown tired of being away from home. His job in the church had changed, too. The Wrights decided to move to a farm near Richmond, Indiana, where Bishop Wright began a church newspaper.

Mrs. Wright's health was not good. She was glad to be near her family. The children saw their grandmother Koerner more often. Grandpa Koerner, who had taught Mrs. Wright her handy skills, had died.

Orville needed money. He had an idea! He would go into the junk business, with Katharine as his partner. Orville and Katharine collected pieces of scrap iron. They took them to the junkyard. Orville liked the junk business better than the old-bone business, especially since he made more money!

One day, Orville watched his friends fly kites. He could not afford to buy a kite, so he built one. To save money, Orville built a kite that was lighter than his friends' kites. His kite flew better than the ones the other boys had bought! Orville's kite flew so well that his friends asked him to make kites for them. Before long, Orville was in the kite-making business. One day, Orville's kite-flying skills would help him unlock the secrets of flying.

Orville had another idea! He decided to go into the chewing gum business. Orville and his friend Harry Morrow mixed tar and sugar to make gum. Of course, they had to test the gum to see if it was any good. Soon, both boys were terribly sick! Whenever he had a chance, Wilbur teased Orville about "that chawin' gum corporation."

Wilbur and Orville began spending more time together. They especially enjoyed the machines and tools in the barn where Grandfather Koerner had built carriages and wagons. They became interested in his lathe, a machine that had a sharp blade that turned and cut wood into special shapes. They pumped a pedal to spin the blade.

Wilbur and Orville decided to build a bigger, faster lathe. They built the pedals so that four boys could spin the blade. To make the blade turn faster, they put clay marbles around the metal bar holding the blade. The boys pumped the pedal. The blade spun faster and faster. The lathe shook. The boys pedaled harder. The barn shook! Then the clay marbles broke, and the lathe ground to a stop. But the barn was still shaking!

Wilbur and Orville heard someone pounding on the barn. It was Katharine, her hair and clothes flying wildly. And the barn was still shaking! The Wright brothers were so busy with their machine that they didn't know they were in a tornado!

In 1883, when Orville was twelve years old, he became fascinated by woodcut prints. He took a broken knife and carved pictures

into pieces of wood. He put ink on the wood and pressed paper onto the ink. When he pulled up the paper, Orville had a picture.

Wilbur was proud of Orville for making woodcuts. That Christmas, Wilbur spent his hard-earned money to buy Orville a special present: a set of carving knives. Orville immediately made new woodcuts. And Bishop Wright let Orville print his woodcuts on the church's printing machine.

In 1884, the Wrights moved back to their beloved house at 7 Hawthorn Street in Dayton. The move came just before Wilbur was to finish high school, so he left without getting his diploma. Later, Wilbur received three honorary college degrees for flying.

Orville missed the last weeks of school, too. He had gotten into trouble, and his sixth-grade teacher, Miss Bond, told him he could not come back to school until he brought his parents to talk with her. But Bishop Wright was out of town, and Mrs. Wright was packing to move to Dayton, so Orville did not tell his parents. He just stayed out of school for the rest of the year!

5
The Wright Brothers' Printing Business

Wilbur and Orville were happy to be back in Dayton. Orville was especially glad to see Ed Sines. He was thrilled to learn that Ed had a toy printing press.

Bishop Wright thought Orville and Ed should have a real printing press. Wilbur and Lorin had built a small rowboat that they never used. Bishop Wright convinced Wilbur and Lorin to trade their rowboat for a printing press. Bishop Wright gave Orville a set of real printing letters to use with his press.

Orville and Ed began a printing company called Sines and Wright. They set up shop in the Wright barn. They advertised that they could "do job printing cheaper than any other house in town." Soon they were printing ads, business cards, tickets, and envelopes.

Ed and Orville enjoyed their printing business. Orville wanted to put the money they made into buying a better printing press. Ed didn't like this idea. The partnership ended when a man paid his printing bill in popcorn. Orville wanted to sell the popcorn for two dollars and spend the money on new letters. Ed wanted to divide the popcorn, pop it, and eat it! Orville had an idea. Ed could have the popcorn if Orville could have the printing business. Ed "sold" his share to Orville. The partnership ended but not the friendship.

Orville moved the printing business to his bedroom. He built a bigger printing press, using an old gravestone! His father gave Orville the job of printing a church pamphlet that Wilbur wrote. Wilbur became a partner in Orville's business. The pamphlet was printed by "Wright Bros. Job Printers, 7 Hawthorn Street." This was the first time

the words "Wright Brothers" were in print. But it wouldn't be the last!

Wilbur was busy, too. He planned to go to college and become a minister. Wilbur took two classes at Central High School and worked with his father on the church paper. He played football, did gymnastics, and was the fastest runner in the school.

That winter, however, Wilbur's life changed. He enjoyed playing ice hockey. One day, a player's stick hit Wilbur in the face. The flying stick knocked out Wilbur's front teeth!

Mrs. Wright took care of Wilbur, but he had other problems. His heart beat too fast. His stomach was upset. Wilbur recovered at home. But the accident left Wilbur unsure of himself.

Orville, however, brimmed with energy and enthusiasm. He was up to his old tricks in school. His teachers put him in the front row to keep an eye on him. He did so well in math that, by eighth grade, Orville was the best math student in Dayton.

Orville wanted a better printing press. Wilbur agreed to help. The Wright brothers built a printing press out of firewood sticks, lumber, and the folding top of an old buggy. The new press was so big that Orville rented a room for it on West Third Street.

One adult printer crawled underneath the printing press to see what the Wright boys had invented. He said, "It works, but I certainly don't see how it does the work."

As Wilbur got better, Mrs. Wright got worse. She stayed in bed. Orville and Katharine were busy at school, and Bishop Wright was away, so Wilbur took care of his mother. He read to her and gave her medicine.

On July 4, 1889, Susan Wright died. Bishop Wright wrote in his journal, "thus went out the light of my home." Bishop Wright knew how well Wilbur had cared for his mother. He said that Wilbur's love and care had kept Mrs. Wright alive two years longer than she might have lived. Wilbur was twenty-two years old and Orville was seventeen when their mother died. Both boys missed their mother. She had been an important part of their lives.

Wilbur again thought about college. Orville became so involved in printing that he worked two summers in a printing shop for no pay.

Orville had another idea! He would print a weekly newspaper called the *West Side News*. Ed Sines sold ads for the paper. Orville printed a story about Abraham Lincoln. Wilbur wrote funny stories. Orville wrote jokes. For example, "What animal falls from the clouds? Reindeer!"

One of Orville's friends, Paul Laurence Dunbar, added poems. Paul Dunbar wrote this poem on the wall of Orville's printing company:

> *Orville Wright is out of sight*
> *In the printing business.*
> *No other mind is half so bright*
> *As his'n is.*

In 1890, with Orville's help, Paul Dunbar began his own newspaper for African-

American readers called *The Tattler.* Paul became a famous African-American poet and author.

Wilbur became the editor of the *West Side News*. He felt better. He had spent the last four years recovering from his accident and caring for his mother. His self-confidence had returned. Wilbur wasn't sure what he would do in the future. Meanwhile, he would work with Orville as his partner.

By 1890, their weekly paper was so popular that Orville and Wilbur decided to print it every day. But competition from bigger Dayton newspapers cut into their profits. Four months later, the Wright brothers stopped printing their paper.

This was not a problem, because the Wright brothers had discovered a new interest: bicycles.

6

The Wright Brothers'
Bicycle Business

Orville once owned a high-wheel bicycle, which had a big wheel in front and a small wheel in back. Orville enjoyed riding his bike around Richmond. A new bicycle, called a safety bike, had been invented in France. The bike was safer because both wheels were the same size.

In 1892, Orville spent $160 for a Columbia safety bike. Wilbur bought a used Columbia bike for $80. Orville began racing his new bike. Wilbur, still cautious after his ice hockey accident, took long rides in the country. Some days Orville joined him.

Wilbur and Orville were often home

alone. Katharine was at college, and Bishop Wright was traveling. They did their own cooking. Orville cooked one week and Wilbur the next week.

The brothers had long discussions. Often they took opposite sides of an argument, then they switched sides and kept talking. Wilbur said, "I love to scrap with Orv!" Their favorite words when they were arguing were "'tis" and "'tisn't." Wilbur and Orville used their wonderful sense of humor to keep their arguments under control.

The young men weren't lonely. Their nieces and nephews lived a few blocks away. Wilbur and Orville played games with them, created toys, flew kites, and made candy. Orville was a candy expert! He made delicious caramels and fudge.

Orville enjoyed teasing the children. His nephew Bus loved mashed potatoes, so Orville played a trick on him. Orville attached a hidden string to Bus's plate. When the bowl of mashed potatoes was put on the table, Orville said, "It seems funny how Bus's plate always makes for the mashed potatoes." Suddenly, Bus's plate began moving toward the bowl! Everyone laughed when they figured out Orville's trick.

Bicycles took more and more of Wilbur's and Orville's time. They enjoyed riding bicycles so much that they decided to sell them.

In December 1892, when Wilbur was twenty-five years old and Orville was twenty-one, they opened their first bicycle shop. The shop was called the Wright Bicycle Exchange. Wilbur ran the store. Orville split his time between his printing business and the new shop. He hired Ed Sines to help with the printing.

The Wright brothers enjoyed selling new bikes, but they especially liked repairing bikes. Soon they had so many bikes to repair that they moved to a bigger shop.

Once, for fun, the Wright brothers took two old high-wheel bikes. They removed the high front wheels and built a bicycle for them both to ride at the same time. People stared when the Wright brothers wobbled

down the street on their high-wheel bicycle built for two!

By 1895, the Wright brothers knew bikes so well that they decided to make their own bicycles. They moved to a new shop they called the Wright Cycle Company.

They named their first handmade model the Van Cleve after their pioneer Van Cleve relatives. A Van Cleve cost $65. Their second bike was the St. Clair and sold for $45. Their third bike, the Wright Special, cost $27.50 in 1897.

The Wright brothers made two major improvements to the design of bicycles. In other bikes, dust got into the ball bearings, making the wheels harder to turn. Wilbur and Orville invented a way to keep dust out of the ball bearings so their wheels rolled more easily.

Their second improvement made pedals safer. The Wright brothers invented pedals that did not fall off.

Wilbur and Orville were busy outside the shop. They held bike races. They entertained their nephews and nieces. Orville learned to play the mandolin. Wilbur learned the harmonica. They built a beautiful wide porch on the Wright house.

They tinkered with projects. Orville improved a friend's adding machine. They made a gas engine to power their tools. When a friend built the first car in Dayton, Orville suggested that he and Wilbur build a car, too. Wilbur didn't think cars had a future. He told Orville, "Why, it would be easier to build a flying machine!"

The bike business was good. Wilbur and Orville, however, were only really busy from spring through summer, when people liked to bike. The rest of the year, things were slow.

The Wright brothers needed something to capture their imagination.

7
Why Not Fly?

In 1896, when he was twenty-five years old, Orville was very sick with typhoid fever and almost died. Wilbur and Katharine cared for him. Wilbur read while sitting with Orville. He read about Otto Lilienthal, who was trying to fly. Lilienthal built gliders and had flown farther than anyone else in the world. But Otto Lilienthal had a gliding accident and died. The Wright brothers were saddened by this news because they admired Mr. Lilienthal and his attempts to fly.

People had long wanted to fly, but no one knew how to build a flying machine. In England, France, the United States, and other countries, people were trying to unlock the mystery of flight.

For the next two years, the Wright brothers talked about flying. But they had the bike shop to run and did not have time to experiment.

In 1899, at age thirty-two, Wilbur read a book about birds. He was bored with bikes and needed to turn his energies to something new. *What about solving the mystery of flying?* he thought.

Wilbur learned all he could about flying. He took every book about it out of the Dayton library. Samuel Langley, the head of the Smithsonian Institution, was trying to learn how to fly. Wilbur decided to write the Smithsonian. A man there sent Wilbur information.

The famous engineer Octave Chanute was also experimenting with gliders. Wilbur wrote him, too. Mr. Chanute quickly became a friend of the Wright brothers.

The Wright brothers rode their bikes in the country to observe birds flying. Buzzards, soaring on the wind without flapping their wings, were their favorite birds.

Wilbur focused on three flying problems. A flying machine needed wings of the right shape to lift a man, power to move the machine through the air, and controls to keep it from crashing. Wilbur and Orville decided that the safest way to discover the best wing shape was to fly kites.

In July 1899, Wilbur built a kite with two wings. Orville was camping, so Wilbur went to a field outside Dayton. Soon Wilbur's kite was soaring, gliding, dipping, and diving. Suddenly, the kite crashed. The kite was a wreck, but Wilbur wasn't disappointed. He had learned how to build a better kite. His new kite would be big enough to carry him into the air!

Wilbur planned to be careful. He knew that the only way to learn how to control a flying machine was to actually go up in it. If his kite could lift him into the air, Wilbur could learn how to steer it. The kite would become a glider.

The Wright brothers decided to not fly their kite near Dayton. The winds weren't strong enough, and there were too many people. The Wrights wanted their flying experiments to be secret.

As usual, Wilbur looked for information. He wrote to the United States Weather Bureau and asked where the strongest winds were. He learned that Kitty Hawk, North Carolina, had everything they needed: strong winds, few people, and soft sand to land on or crash in!

In August 1900, the Wright brothers began building their kite. They made wooden and metal parts in their bicycle shop. They sewed cloth for the wings on the sewing machine at home. The Wright house was in an uproar, getting the brothers and the flying machine ready.

The biggest problem they faced was how to keep the wings from tipping and making the glider crash. One day, Wilbur was twisting an empty cardboard box. He noticed something important. When he twisted the box, one end bent up, and the other end bent down. If they could make the glider wings do the same thing, they would have solved a big problem in controlling their glider. They tested Wilbur's idea on a kite, and it worked!

8

Kitty Hawk

On September 3, 1900, Wilbur told his father he was taking the flying machine to Kitty Hawk. Orville would join him, and they would fly!

Wilbur carefully packed the pieces of the flying machine in crates and set out on September 6, 1900. He rode the train for two days, took a steamship, rowed in a leaky boat, and sailed until he reached Kitty Hawk. The Kitty Hawk folks were friendly, but they wondered what Wilbur was up to.

Wilbur worked on the flying machine. On September 23, Wilbur wrote his father, "I do not intend to take dangerous chances, both because I have no wish to get hurt and because a fall would stop my experiment-ing."

Orville joined Wilbur on September 28. They set up their tent and finished building their glider. On October 3, the wind was strong and steady. The Wright brothers soon had their flying machine flying. It dipped and soared as they pulled its ropes. They were excited about what they were learning.

They knew the only way to understand flying was to fly. Wilbur would go up. Orville and Bill Tate, a Kitty Hawk friend, held the ropes. Wilbur held on to the flying machine. Slowly, the kite took off. Wilbur flew to a height of fifteen feet until the kite bobbed up and down!

"Let me down!" Wilbur yelled. Orville and Bill tugged on the ropes. The flying machine glided down onto the soft sand.

"I promised Pop I'd take care of myself," Wilbur said with a smile. Wilbur and Orville experimented with their kite, but without Wilbur hanging on. They put chains on it to

test how much weight the glider could carry. When it crashed, they repaired it. Tom Tate, Bill Tate's young nephew, flew. He didn't weigh much and gave good reports.

Wilbur wanted to glide now. The Wright brothers had learned how their machine flew as a kite. They took their flying machine down the beach to the Kill Devil Hills. Here, they could get a running start and glide down the long hills.

On October 18, Wilbur glided for one hundred feet. He stayed in the air for fifteen seconds! Even though he could have flown farther, Wilbur gently landed the glider. This time he had flown without any ropes!

The Wright brothers had accomplished all they set out to do. They would return to Dayton to build an even better flying machine.

The Wright brothers took their flying machine to a hilltop and let it fly into the air on its own. The glider crashed, and they left it.

Mrs. Tate cut the cloth from the wings

and made dresses for her daughters. She wouldn't let such good material be wasted!

The materials for the first Wright glider cost Wilbur and Orville fifteen dollars. The knowledge they gained was priceless.

That winter, the Wright brothers built a bigger glider. They wanted the pilot to guide it with a steering rudder.

They returned to Kitty Hawk in July 1901 with the biggest glider ever built. They built two wooden sheds: one to live in and the other for their flying machine. They didn't want the tricky wind to fly their glider when they weren't watching.

There were other things flying at Kitty Hawk. Millions of mosquitoes attacked them daily. Orville wrote Katharine, "There was no escape. They chewed us clean through our underwear and socks."

The determined brothers didn't give up. On July 27, 1901, Wilbur flew in the glider seventeen times. But something was still wrong. The glider flew fine for a few seconds, then it bucked up and came down.

They understood now how Otto Lilienthal had been killed. Fortunately, the soft sand kept Wilbur from being hurt.

As usual, the Wright brothers studied the problem. They changed the wings. Success! Wilbur was able to better control the glider. Soon, he was gliding distances of four hundred feet.

The Wright brothers wanted even better control, however. Their flying machine frequently crashed. Each time, they repaired it after trying to figure out what went wrong.

By August, they were discouraged, even though they had set the record for the world's longest glide. Their flying machine still crashed. Something was wrong, but they did not know what it was.

Wilbur wrote, "We doubted we would ever resume our experiments."

Wilbur told Orville, "Not within a thousand years would man ever fly."

Wilbur Wright was wrong.

9
First Flight

The Wright brothers' friend Octave Chanute still had faith in them. He asked Wilbur to give a speech about flying.

Wilbur, dressed in Orville's best clothes, gave his speech in Chicago on September 18, 1901. He was a success! Best of all, Wilbur once again had faith in their ideas. He also knew how to solve the wing problems.

The Wright brothers needed to know how wings worked in the wind. It took too much time to build gliders and experiment, so they built a long box called a wind tunnel. They created a steady wind in the tunnel with a fan. They tested wings of all shapes and sizes. They worked out the math of wings in wind.

The wing formation they had been using was wrong! By Christmas, they had solved the problem.

Now they knew they could build a better flying machine. That winter, they talked and argued and built their new glider. The wings and the steering rudder were different. They still built bicycles, because they needed money. But every extra minute and penny went into their new flying machine.

In July 1902, the Wright brothers returned to Kitty Hawk with their new glider. They were amazed at how well it flew. They made flights lasting almost a minute. They flew distances of six hundred feet. Every once in a while, the glider suddenly crashed into the sand. They called these crashes "welldiggers."

Orville had an idea! The steering rudder in the back of the glider had to move. If the pilot could move the rudder better, he could stop the crashes. Orville solved the problem. The glider stopped crashing.

The Wright brothers needed an engine to power their machine. With an engine, they would be the first people to really fly.

Back in Dayton, they went to work. They needed at least an eight-horsepower motor that weighed less than two hundred pounds. No such motor existed, so they built one with the help of their friend Charlie Taylor. Their motor was loud, but it weighed only 170 pounds and created twelve horsepower.

Next, they needed a propeller to pull the glider through the air. They tested different propellers in their wind tunnel until they had a shape that worked. All spring, they carefully made the pieces of their new flying machine, which they called the Wright Flyer. In September 1903, Wilbur and Orville took off for Kitty Hawk again.

The brothers spent three weeks building their new flying machine. They tested the propellers and motor. Suddenly, the propeller shaft shook so much it bent. They sent it to Charlie Taylor in Dayton to fix. While they waited, the Wright brothers hunted, argued, and laughed. Orville played his mandolin. Wilbur blew his harmonica.

When the shaft was sent back, they tried again. The shaft still shook, so Orville went to Dayton to make a stronger one.

Finally, on December 11, Orville returned. By December 15, 1903, the flying machine was ready. The Wright brothers were ready. But who would be the first to fly?

They decided to flip a coin. The winner would be first. Wilbur won! He would be the first man to fly an airplane. The motor sputtered and roared to life. Wilbur climbed on and lay down. The Wright Flyer rolled down the track they had laid on the sand. Wilbur was so eager he steered the flying machine up too soon. He crashed. The airplane was slightly damaged. So was Wilbur's pride.

The brothers repaired their airplane. On December 17, 1903, the Wright Flyer was ready to fly again.

It was Orville's turn. The motor started. The propellers spun. The flying machine rolled down the track. Orville pulled on the

controls. Slowly, the Wright Flyer lifted off into the air. Orville was flying!

Orville soared a distance of 120 feet. He was in the air for twelve seconds. His flight wasn't very long, but it was the first time anyone had ever flown a powered machine.

The Wright brothers had made history! They would be famous around the world.

They flew three more times. Wilbur set the record of 852 feet. He stayed in the air for fifty-nine seconds. No one had ever flown that long or that far before!

The excited Wright brothers stopped to discuss what adjustments were needed to make an even longer flight. Suddenly, the wind sent the Flyer tumbling down the beach. The first airplane was wrecked!

Wilbur and Orville collected the pieces. They were disappointed they couldn't fly anymore. But they were thrilled to know that they had flown. They knew they would make many, many more flights in the future.

10
Wilbur and Orville Fly
Into History

Everyone at 7 Hawthorn Street was excited when the Wright brothers arrived home on December 23, 1903. They talked about their flights. They discussed what they had learned. Bishop Wright and Katharine shared Wilbur and Orville's enthusiasm. The Wright brothers had reached their goal. As they talked, Orville drank seven glasses of milk! He hadn't been able to find fresh milk in Kitty Hawk.

The Wright brothers enjoyed their success, but they were eager to build a better airplane. On January 1, 1904, they began working on a new plane. By spring, the flying machine was ready.

They needed a place to fly. Kitty Hawk was too far away. They wanted a place close to home that was near a train and that could provide privacy.

Katharine and Orville remembered Huffman's Field, where they had gone on science trips in high school. The field was open, near train tracks, and was surrounded by a hedge.

The Wright brothers asked Mr. Huffman if they could use his field. Mr. Huffman agreed, but only if his horses and cows were safely out of the field. Wilbur and Orville cut the tall grass by hand. They built a shed. By the middle of April, they were building a flying machine at Huffman's Field.

On May 23, 1904, forty people came to watch them fly. But the flying machine had a motor problem. Everyone went home disappointed.

Wilbur and Orville didn't give up. All summer, they worked on their airplane.

Sometimes it flew a little. Sometimes it didn't. Sometimes it crashed. They finally figured out they needed more speed to take off. They built a catapult to launch the flying machine into the air. Once again, the Wright brothers faced a difficult problem and solved it.

On September 20, Orville flew a complete circle over the field. His flight was almost a mile long and lasted one minute thirty-five seconds — a new world record. By December, they were able to fly five circles and stay in the air for five minutes.

The Wright brothers worked on perfecting their airplane. The governments of the United States, France, and England wanted to buy Wright Flyers.

The Wright brothers had their ups and downs. Their airplanes were better, but other people took their ideas and flew, too.

In 1908, Wilbur flew in France. His wide circles and long flights made newspaper headlines. A French reporter wrote, "Yes! I have today seen Wilbur Wright and his great white bird . . . there is no doubt! Wilbur and

Orville Wright have well and truly flown."
An English newspaper's headline called their
plane "THE MOST WONDERFUL FLYING-MACHINE
THAT HAS EVER BEEN BUILT."

While Wilbur was in France, Orville was in
America, setting world records for long flights.
In September he flew for seventy minutes. He
even took passengers up with him.

Then, on September 17, disaster struck.
Orville went up with Lieutenant Thomas
Selfridge. Suddenly, something snapped, and
the airplane crashed. Orville lived, but Lieutenant Selfridge died. He was the first person
to die in a powered airplane crash.

Orville had done nothing wrong. A propeller broke and caused the plane to crash.
Orville was in the hospital for seven weeks.
Katharine took care of him. In France, Wilbur was setting records and winning prizes
for distance and height.

In January 1909, Orville and Katharine
joined Wilbur in France. Orville could walk
with the help of two canes. After his acci-

dent, Orville rarely flew again. The bumpiness was too painful.

Kings and queens watched Wilbur fly. The Wright brothers received medals and prizes. France gave Katharine a medal of honor for helping her famous brothers.

When the Wright brothers came home to Dayton, ten thousand people cheered them. While pleased with the attention, the Wright brothers slipped away to work on airplanes in their bicycle shop.

President William Howard Taft invited the Wright brothers to the White House. President Taft said, "You made this discovery by keeping your nose right at the job until you had accomplished what you had determined to do."

On June 18, 1909, there was a great homecoming celebration in Dayton. Hundreds of children dressed in red, white, and blue formed a "living" American flag. There were speeches, parades, and fireworks. Wilbur and Orville slipped away as soon as they could. There was work to do. Early the next morning, they took a train to demonstrate their airplane to the army.

The Wright brothers worked on their airplanes for the next three years. In 1912, Wilbur got typhoid fever. On May 30, 1912, Wilbur Wright died. Orville, Katharine, and Bishop Wright were with him. Wilbur was only forty-five years old. Bishop Wright wrote in his daily diary, "Seeing the right clearly, pursuing steadfastly, he lived and died."

A thousand telegrams arrived from all over the world. Twenty-five thousand people walked past Wilbur's coffin. Orville worked on airplanes the rest of his life. He died on January 30, 1948, when he was seventy-six years old. Orville had lived long enough to see airplanes circle the earth and people dream of flying into space.

When Wilbur and Orville were born, no one imagined that the Wright brothers would be the first to fly.